Dolphins

Steve Parish

ANIMALS are Fun!

Library of Congress Cataloging-in-Publication Data

Lever, E. Melanie.
    Dolphins / text by E. Melanie Lever, Kate Lovett, and Pat Slater; photographs by Steve Parish.
        p. cm. — (Animals are fun!)
    Includes index.
    Summary: Text and photographs present the life cycle, habits, and physical characteristics of dolphins.
        ISBN 0-8368-2612-4 (lib. bdg.)
        1. Dolphins—Juvenile literature. [1. Dolphins.] I. Lovett, Kate. II. Slater, Pat.
III. Parish, Steve, ill. IV. Title.
QL737.C432L48   2000
599.53—dc21   99-054138

First published in North America in 2000 by
Gareth Stevens Publishing
330 West Olive Street, Suite 100
Milwaukee, WI 53212 USA

This edition © 2000 by Gareth Stevens, Inc.. First published in 1998 by Steve Parish Publishing Pty. Ltd., P. O. Box 1058, Archerfield, BC, Queensland 4108, Australia. Original edition © 1998 by Steve Parish Publishing Pty. Ltd. Photography and creative direction by Steve Parish. Text by E. Melanie Lever, Kate Lovett, and Pat Slater, SPP. Additional end matter © 2000 by Gareth Stevens, Inc.

U.S. author: Amy Bauman

Printed in the United States of America

2 3 4 5 6 7 8 9 05 04 03 02 01

Gareth Stevens Publishing
A WORLD ALMANAC EDUCATION GROUP COMPANY

The dolphin is a warm-blooded mammal that lives in the ocean.

A dolphin breathes air through a blowhole on top of its head.

The dolphin uses its excellent hearing to locate objects.

It makes many types of sounds
as it searches the water for food.

The sounds echo, or bounce back, from the food to the dolphin.

With its little, pointed teeth,
a dolphin grabs fish to eat.

The dolphin moves its tail up and down, not side to side like a fish.

A dolphin "pops" its head out of the water to see things.

A female dolphin has a baby every two to three years.

Each of the baby dolphins
is born under water.

Dolphins live together in groups called schools or pods.

Some of the pods contain hundreds of dolphins.

Dolphins are usually very friendly animals.